# THE CAKE CAFÉ BAKE BOOK

# CAKE

When writing for this book I started to think about what I enjoy about the work I do in the Café and what matters to me the most in my day-to-day life. There are so many things — my husband (of course), my family and friends, travel, my work, food, my writing, my social life, my city, my home, my house, art. They are all hugely important and then it dawned on me that what is even more important than having these things in my life, is trying to balance them all.

I love living in Dublin and created a business here to give myself a lifestyle that I enjoy. In the Café I get to chat with customers, get to know their day to day, watch the local children progress from christening cakes, to each birthday cake to an after school treat. In the past five years I hope that the Café has become a neighborhood staple, a place that is embedded in the conscience of the customers, as much a part of the city as the Forty Foot or Busáras. In some ways I feel this has worked and in others it has surpassed anything I could have ever hoped. We were featured in *Vogue* — how much better does it get for a girl than that?

When I opened The Cake Café, at first, life slipped out of balance quite sharply. I had no business experience but I do know that I am not the world's best employee, so I decided to set up my own business and work for myself. The first years were draining and exhausting but it worked. I worked harder and harder and it all eventually became easier. I am sure I tried my husband's patience, I definitely slipped out of touch with friends, and I no longer had time to spend a day wandering around art galleries.

There is no question that it would be very tempting to put all of my energy into work but at the end of the day it is time spent on other things that makes me a happy person and helps me to be more creative in my life.

# & COFFEE

One defining moment taught me the importance
of creating this balance. My father died, very suddenly,
almost ten years ago. His death made me understand how
fragile life is and the essential need for equilibrium hit me
full force. Losing a loved one helped me to better focus
on what it is that is most important to me and why I enjoy
baking, cooking and the community
that the Café has developed.

If you are not used to baking, it takes time and a little
patience, but that does not mean it is rocket science either.
I firmly believe in making life as easy as possible for myself
and there are plenty of baking tips that can help you to
streamline the way you do things. For example, you can
make a big batch of biscuit dough, roll it into a log, cut it and
then freeze the slices. Pastry can also be frozen, rolled out to
the size you want or in a block. Bun batter can be stored
in a fridge for a day or two before use,
and scooped out into bun cases as needed.

As with pretty much everything we eat, the quality of the
ingredients used filters down to the final taste. I would
recommend investing in real butter and good, fresh,
free-range eggs. We use all natural flavouring in our cakes,
the fresh zest of a lemon, our own café-made vanilla extract
and good, strong coffee. I feel baking is a treat
but it can still be good for your body.

At The Cake Café, we specialise in good quality
home baking rather than fancy, intricate cakes, and all of
these recipes are ones we use on a day-to-day basis.
I hope you enjoy this book, eat well
and bake something great.

—Michelle Darmody

I DON'T REALLY GET FOOD. You know, it's fine. I get that it's important from a survival point of view, that without it I'd just lie on the couch in my underpants all day weeping at old episodes of Cash In The Attic, or gazing lustily at the houses one with the lady that I secretly fancy. But as an entity in itself, there are so many other things that I prefer to food: bicycles, sport generally (except horse racing), talking about sport, music, dogs, books, tales of Antarctic exploration, Christopher Hitchens YouTube clips, pitch & putt. Food takes too long. Too long to get ready, too long to come to the table. Then a further delay while you wait for those with inferior shoveling actions wolf it down. Because you have to sit there, because that is the rule, written in the stupid crappy book of the rules of food that nobody has ever seen.

I've been to some very fancy restaurants. Ones where they unfold your napkin for you and drape it across your nuts like the lead thing when you get a chest x-ray. And it was fine. Absolutely fine. Fine, fine, fine. But nowhere near as tasty/delicious/enjoyable as peanut butter on multigrain toast when you get home and you're drunk. I'm not being whimsical or glib or anything here. That is what I judge all food against. That is the Nabokov of cooking. The culinary Amundsen (inappropriate ref. as I believe he ate some of his dogs on the way back from the pole). The point is, I have eaten ten slices of decadently peanut buttered toast in a row (5 × 2), standing there, staring at the toaster, willing the next couple to surface. I once went to sleep, sat on the floor of my parents' kitchen, hammered, with my face in a plate of heavily peanut buttered toast. I very much doubt I'll ever meet another meal I am willing to be as intimate with.

I have a strange job. I'm either somewhere else, saying jokes to strangers, or I'm walking around Dublin, trying to think of new ones. Lunch was always a disruption. It usually involved a distance of bread, stuffed with a foliage that tasted less dull, that I could eat while I walked — *flâneured* — around the city, mumbling junk into my phone or scrawling it on my hand.

But then I moved in around the corner from The Cake Café. I mean it is still just food, but now I seem to turn up there most days. I sit down while I eat it. Sometimes I think I may even enjoy it. I'm not sure what's going on. They seem to be on to something.

—David O'Doherty

When I decided to publish a little book, I could think of no one better to ask for an introduction than David O'Doherty. Not only is he a world-class funny man, but also one of our favorite customers at the Café ...

# PEANUT BUTTER &TOAST

# T O A S T

So this method might not be as quick as David's but it will give you a very tasty peanut butter on multi-seed toast. I really like the squish of a warm raisin with the salty crunch of peanut butter so I would probably throw a handful of raisins into the dough mix as well.

| oven | 210°C | 410°F G6 |
|---|---|---|
| 2lb loaf tin, oiled & warmed | | |
| strong white flour | 400g | 14oz |
| coarse wholemeal flour | 50g | 1¾oz |
| salt | 1lvltsp | 1lvltsp |
| sugar | 1.3tsp | 1⅓tsp |
| fresh yeast | 20g | ¾oz |
| warm water | 300ml | 10floz |
| sunflower seeds | 40g | 1½oz |
| pumpkin seeds | 40g | 1½oz |
| raisins | handful | handful |

Put all ingredients into the mixer. Use the dough hook on the slowest setting until all the flour is combined. Then turn the mixer to medium and leave to work away for 12 minutes, or knead by hand for about the same amount of time, until the dough is smooth to the touch.

Put the dough in a lightly-oiled dish and cover with a damp cloth. The cloth should cover the dish but not touch the dough. Leave the bowl somewhere warm without any draughts until it has doubled in size, which should take just under an hour.

After the hour, knead the dough lightly. Form into a tight loaf shape, and put into the warmed and oiled 2lb loaf tin. Let it proof for another fifteen minutes.

**bake                    25min**

The top should be golden and base should sound hollow when you tap it.

# P E A N U T  B U T T E R

I use roasted and lightly salted peanuts to make this nut butter. You can experiment with other nuts too.

| peanuts | 350g | 12oz |
|---|---|---|
| very light olive oil | 1tbsp | 1tbsp |
| sugar | 1tsp | 1tsp |

Blitz the peanuts until they are beginning to break up. Add the oil and sugar and blend until it is as chunky or smooth as you desire. Then, follow David's recipe: get drunk, make toast ...

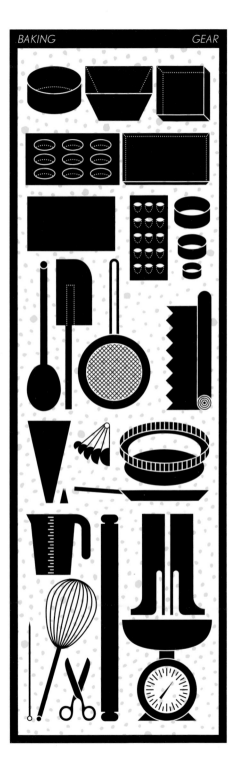

The recipes in this book should all be easy enough to make at home no matter how large or small your kitchen. There is no particularly specialist equipment needed, they are good old-fashioned, hearty cakes that require a little time and a bit of love but no frills and fancy bits.

This section outlines all the equipment and know-how you need to create all of the recipes in this book. You do not need to run out and grab everything straight away. Have a look over the recipes in the book that you like, gather together what is necessary for those particular cakes and start from there.

If you are anything like me you will flick through the book and take a few recipes from it; make them your own and use them as your party pieces again and again. I love getting familiar with a recipe and getting to a stage where I almost know it by heart. My mother bakes like this; I see her instinctively making a perfect batch of scones with just a mere glance at a recipe. She has years of practice baking for a hungry brood of children and their assorted entourages.

# BAKE

Many people are scared of baking, but it does not need to be as difficult as you would think. Yes, sifting flour makes a lighter cake, but it will still work out if you don't. I have tried to simplify the recipes in this book. There are a few tips below that will help you along the way, but if you start to bake regularly you will soon find your own path.

## GEAR

Of course, a mixer does make baking much easier, as it is often necessary to mix cakes or knead dough thoroughly, and for a bit of time. In saying this you can always use old-fashioned elbow grease and a wooden spoon, and in most circumstances a hand whisk will also work.

| cake tins | 2lb loaf tin |
| --- | --- |
| | 8" round spring-form |
| | 9" square |
| | bun tray |
| | Swiss roll tin, about 11×7" |
| | 8" tart tin with removable base |
| other gear | baking tray |
| | round cutters |
| | sieve |
| | wooden spoon |
| | spatula |
| | weighing scales |
| | grater / zester / microplane |
| | skewer |
| | whisk (or mixer or hand whisk) |
| | rolling pin (or heavy bottle) |
| | baking parchment |
| | piping bag and star nozzle |
| | oven dish (like for lasagne) |
| | frying pan |
| | wire rack |
| | measuring jug |

## TEMPERATURE

Ingredients should be at room temperature unless otherwise stated. Always preheat your oven; it should be at the stated temperature before you put the cake into it. Oven temperatures throughout this book are for an oven with a fan.

## YOUR OVEN

You may need to take time to get to know your oven. Ovens can vary greatly depending on whether they have a fan or not, whether they are old or new. If your cake does not work out perfectly the first time do not get disheartened. You can adjust your oven the next time. Some ovens have hot spots so you may need to alternate the position of trays in the oven during the second half of the baking time. If you still have your manufacturer's booklet it may provide you with some help.

## MIXING

It is best to start your mixer on a low speed to begin. Once the ingredients are combined you can then turn up the speed and beat the mix for the required time. I usually turn the mixer up a little higher for a sponge cake to get it nice and fluffy and full of bubbles. Folding is a method of adding ingredients so you preserve the air bubbles.

## LINING AND GREASING

It may seem like a pain but it is worth your while to take a little time to line and grease your tins. We use baking parchment for all our lining.

LINING A ROUND TIN

To grease a tin you can either use oil or butter. I tend to use the old fashioned method I was taught as a child. As butter comes wrapped in foil paper, I rip off a piece and rub it onto the cake tin. A pastry brush dipped in melted butter can also be used. Just a thin layer. You do not want to add too much extra butter or oil to the cake — this is especially true with biscuits as too much greasing can make them burn on the base. Sometimes we just line the tin, sometimes we grease first and then line — we have noted what we find best for each recipe. For pastry, it is best to grease the tin and then lightly flour it.

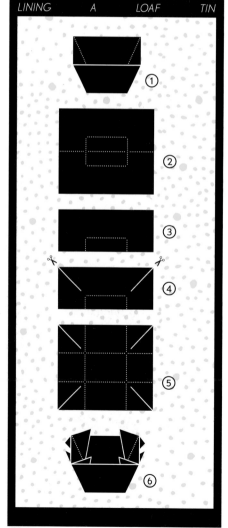

LINING A LOAF TIN

## DONENESS
To test that a cake is perfectly cooked, you should insert a skewer into the centre of it. If the skewer comes out with some cake mix attached you need to leave the cake in the oven a little longer. When the cake is ready there should be no mix on the skewer (though this does not count for brownies, as you want those to be gooey and sticky). If a cake sinks in the middle after you have removed it from the oven it generally means it has been undercooked. If it sinks while it is still in the oven it can mean that the oven was too hot, the cake rising too quickly and then collapsing. If the cake cracks a lot, it may also mean that the oven was too hot. If any of the above happens to you, do not panic! As long as it is not burnt or raw the cake will probably still taste good, perhaps not exactly as you had hoped, but still tasty. At The Cake Café we generally turn a cake upside down before icing it. You can disguise a lot of things with your approach to icing!

## COOLING
Leave cakes in the tin until they are warm enough to handle, then gently remove them and allow to cool on a wire rack. Similarly, biscuits harden perfectly if carefully taken from their baking tray and placed on a wire rack.

## MEASURING
Place your measuring container for liquids on a flat surface and always check at eye level. 'Spoon' measures are all given here as round measurements unless otherwise stated. This means you fill the spoon so the ingredient's raised surface is approximately the same size as that of the base of the spoon. A heaped spoon means there is as much of the ingredient crammed on the spoon as will fit. A level spoon means you push some back off with your finger so the spoon is just covered. Though most people will probably not have a tablespoon to hand, it is simply the size of two dessert spoons.

| | |
|---|---|
| teaspoon | tsp |
| tablespoon | tbsp |
| dessertspoon | dstsp |
| heaped | hpd |
| level | lvl |

## BUTTER
Butter should be at room temperature but not so soft that it is beginning to melt, as melted butter will alter the texture of the cake you are baking. There are a few recipes where cold butter is asked for, particularly in pastry or scones. If this is the case the butter is best cut into cubes before being added to the mix. Cold butter helps to make the pastry crispy.

## EGGS

Eggs should not be used straight from the fridge but at room temperature. We use medium sized, free-range eggs in all our recipes. When using raw eggs please be very careful and make sure they are really fresh.

## CHOCOLATE

All of the chocolate that we use in the Café comes in small chocolate chips which makes it very easy to melt. We use chocolate with 70% cocoa solids. If you do not have chips just break a bar into pieces about the the size of a small coin.

## SUGAR

We use castor sugar (also spelled "caster"). It's a finer version of granulated sugar. You can make it by blitzing granulated sugar in a blender. It melts easier and works better in most recipes.

## VANILLA SUGAR

Great for dusting on sponge cakes or sprinkling on biscuits.

| | | |
|---|---|---|
| icing sugar | 250g | 8½oz |
| vanilla pods | 1 sliced lengthwise | |

Place the sugar and vanilla into an airtight container and it will last for a few months.

## VANILLA EXTRACT

At the Café we use quite a bit of vanilla extract, so we decided to make our own. It is really simple and much more cost effective than using shop-bought. We make this by the litre but I have scaled the recipe down for home use.

| | |
|---|---|
| vodka | 1 naggin (200ml) |
| vanilla pods | 3 |

Take a clean bottle and fill it with the vodka. Slice the vanilla pods in half length ways, so you can see the lovely sticky black seeds inside. Place the sliced pods into the vodka and leave for about three months or until the liquid goes black. You now have your very own vanilla extract. During baking the alcohol in the extract will evaporate leaving the lovely vanilla flavour behind to add richness to your cakes and biscuits.

## ALLERGIES

More and more people are becoming aware of their allergies. At the Café, we have been particularly working on recipes that contain no flour, as this is what we are most regularly asked for. Be careful when cooking with nuts if anyone you might be serving has a nut allergy, and dairy can cause dietary problems for many people. I have included a few recipes that are dairy free, with oil being generally used in its place. Soya milk can almost always be used in place of ordinary milk.

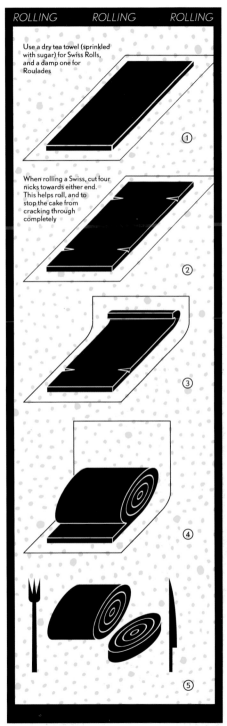

ROLLING     ROLLING     ROLLING

Use a dry tea towel (sprinkled with sugar) for Swiss Rolls, and a damp one for Roulades

①

When rolling a Swiss, cut four nicks towards either end. This helps roll, and to stop the cake from cracking through completely

②

③

④

⑤

# SCONES

Makes ten large scones or twice that if you use a small cutter. Adjust your oven times a minute or two either way, depending on the size you make.

| | | | |
|---|---|---|---|
| **makes** | **10 (large)** | | |
| **oven** | **200°C** | **390°F** | **G5** |
| **baking tray, lined with baking parchment** | | | |
| **plain flour** | **450g** | **1lb** | |
| **salt** | **1lvltsp** | **1lvltsp** | |
| **baking soda** | **2lvltsp** | **2lvltsp** | |
| **cream of tartar** | **4lvltsp** | **4lvltsp** | |
| **cold butter** | **80g** | **3oz** | |
| **castor sugar** | **80g** | **3oz** | |
| **eggs** | **2** | **2** | |
| **buttermilk** *added to* *eggs to make total of* | **300ml** | **10½ floz** | |

Mix dry ingredients and rub in the butter then stir in the sugar.

Lightly mix the eggs and milk and add to mixture.

As with pastry, the less you handle the scone dough the lighter the scones will be. The mixture should be soft but not sticky. Turn out onto a lightly-floured surface and pat to about an inch and a half thickness. Cut with cutter, or an upside down glass, and place them apart on the baking tray. Be careful not to twist the cutter too much as you press down or it will cause the scones to rise unevenly.

**bake**                  **20min**
… until risen and golden.

You can add many things to this basic recipe. We most often add raisins for fruit scones, but you could chop up any other dried fruit or nuts, even add chocolate chips if you like. Some small cubes of pear and a drop of vanilla extract are a great alternative. If you do not have cream of tartar and baking soda you can substitute them with the same total quantity of baking powder. If you do this, use milk instead of buttermilk.

Scones are one of my favorite ways to start the day. I love to take one when they are just out of the oven — so tantalisingly warm — and you have to juggle it between your fingers. I smother it in butter, which melts down through the lovely bread, and then top it with a dollop of homemade jam. Or, if I have some on hand, whipped cream instead of the butter. Or both…

# SCONES

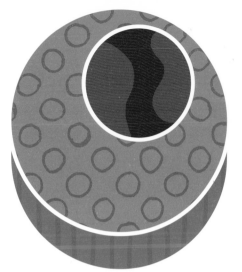

# BROWN SCONES

| | | |
|---|---|---|
| makes | 10 | |
| oven | 200°C | 390°F G5 |
| baking tray, lined with baking parchment | | |

| | | |
|---|---|---|
| plain flour | 140g | 5oz |
| wholemeal flour | 280g | 10oz |
| bread soda | 1 lvltsp | 1 lvltsp |
| baking powder | ¼ lvltsp | ¼ lvltsp |
| salt pinch | 1 | 1 |
| cold butter | 60g | 2oz |
| honey | 2tsp | 2tsp |
| eggs, beaten | 2 | 2 |
| milk *added to* | | |
| *eggs to make total of* | ½ **pint** | 280ml |

Mix dry ingredients and rub in the butter.

Lightly mix the egg, milk and honey and add to mixture.

Turn out onto a lightly floured surface and pat to about an inch and a half thickness. Cut with cutter and place apart on baking tray.

| | |
|---|---|
| **bake** | **15–20min** |

... until golden.

# DROP SCONES

| | | |
|---|---|---|
| makes | 12 | |
| frying pan | | |

| | | |
|---|---|---|
| eggs, separated | 2 | 2 |
| cream cheese | 100g | 3.5oz |
| vanilla extract | 1tsp | 1tsp |
| milk | 100mls | 3.5floz |
| self-raising flour | 60g | 2oz |
| ground cinnamon | 1tsp | 1tsp |
| butter | knob | knob |

Whisk the egg whites until stiff and fluffy. I pour a very small drop of vinegar onto some paper towel and rub the inside of the bowl to remove any oil that might have been in the bowl. If there is any fat such as oil or egg yolk in egg whites they will not get as light and fluffy as they should.

Mix together the egg yolks with the vanilla, cream cheese and milk.

Sieve the flour with the cinnamon into the bowl of egg yolks and stir well.

Fold in the egg white.

Melt the butter in a pan and drop a spoon-full of batter into the butter. Turn over when you see the edges turning golden.

These are lovely served with a blueberry compote or any fruit compote for that matter.

# J A M
# T A R T S

| makes | 16 | | |
|---|---|---|---|
| oven | 180°C | 350°F | G4 |
| bun tray, greased & flour dusted | | | |

| | | |
|---|---|---|
| runny jam | 12tsp | 12tsp |
| plain flour | 225g | 8oz |
| cold butter | 140g | 5oz |
| castor sugar | 55g | 2oz |
| eggs | 1 | 1 |
| salt pinch | 1 | 1 |

Mix the flour and salt. Rub in butter, do not overmix. Stir the sugar into the egg, mix it lightly and add to the flour.

**rest pastry in fridge**    **3hrs** *or* **overnight**

Roll the pastry on a flour-dusted surface and cut into circles large enough to fit into the holes in the tray.

Gently place them in the bun tray and place a small spoon of jam in the centre. Leave room all around so that the jam does not spill over while baking.

Cover the top if you wish. I like to create a lattice with thin strips of pastry or to cut out pastry stars and pop them on top.

| bake | 15min |
|---|---|
| cool | 20min |
| eat | all |

Small, sticky, easy, tasty, sugary, sweet and neat — buns and tarts are perfectly formed cakes for those who do not want to share.

# B U N S &
# T A R T S

# FAIRY CAKES

These are very versatile cakes and are extremely easy to serve. You do not need a knife or fork, just your hands and the whole cake is all for you. The batter can be kept in the fridge for a day or two. I find an ice cream scoop is the perfect way to measure the amount of batter for our bun cases.

| makes | 12 | |
|---|---|---|
| oven | 180°C | 350°F G4 |
| bun tray, bun cases | | |
| butter | 225g | 8oz |
| castor sugar | 225g | 8oz |
| self-raising flour | 225g | 8oz |
| eggs | 4 | 4 |
| vanilla extract | 0.5tsp | ½tsp |
| *or* | | |
| lemon zest | 1 | 1 |

Place cases into bun tray.

Mix the eggs and vanilla in a jug separate to the mixing bowl, we use a measuring jug for ease of pouring.

Beat butter and sugar until light and fluffy. Slowly add the egg mix, if it begins to curdle add a small bit of the flour then continue adding the eggs.

Add in flour. Make sure you stop the mixer and scrape the sides of the bowl a few times. This helps to completely combine the batter.

Scoop the mixture into the cases and pop them into a preheated oven.

| bake | 15min |
|---|---|

# OVERNIGHT GRANOLA BUNS

WHEAT FREE

| makes | 12 | |
|---|---|---|
| oven | 180°C | 350°F G4 |
| bun tray, greased & flour dusted | | |
| spelt flour | 185g | 6½oz |
| granola | 160g | 5½oz |
| ground cinnamon | 1tsp | 1tsp |
| ground ginger | 1tsp | 1tsp |
| orange zest | 2 | 2 |
| ground cardamon | 1tsp | 1tsp |
| bread soda | 1tsp | 1tsp |
| brown sugar | 100g | 3½oz |
| bran | 30g | 1oz |
| dates, stoned | 120g | 4¼oz |
| buttermilk | 370ml | 12½floz |
| olive oil | 120ml | 4floz |
| eggs, beaten | 1 | 1 |

Mix all of the ingredients together in a large bowl. Cover with clingfilm and place in the fridge overnight.

Divide the mixture between the holes in the tin.

| bake | 20min |
|---|---|

*BUNS & TARTS*

# ECLAIRS

These were considered very fancy in our house when we were small. They were baked when very special guests would be coming to visit. I guess they are a little more fiddly than other recipes in the book so they take a little extra time and a strong arm. The pastry can turn into a slippery little bugger when you are adding the eggs so beware and use a large pot.

| | | | |
|---|---|---|---|
| makes | 12 | | |
| oven | 220°C | 425°F | G7 |
| baking tray, lined with baking parchment | | | |

| | | |
|---|---|---|
| water | 140ml | ¼ pint |
| butter, cubed | 50g | 2oz |
| plain flour, sieved | 100g | 4oz |
| eggs | 3 | 3 |
| cream | 250ml | ½ pint |

Pour the water and butter into a saucepan and bring to a brisk boil. You will be using the saucepan when you mix in all the other ingredients so use one big enough to accommodate.

Tip all of the flour into the saucepan at once and beat until the mixture has completely combined and the sides of the pan are clean. Then continue beating for one minute over the heat.

Take the pastry off the heat and beat in the eggs one at a time until the mixture is smooth and glossy. Beat for about two minutes for each egg. Often two and a half eggs will do. This hurts your arms but believe me if you do not beat it like mad you will not have light and fluffy cakes.

The pastry should be thick enough to hold its shape when piped.

Scoop the mixture into a piping bag with a plain tube and pipe twelve lengths just longer than your middle finger. Leave a bit of room between each one as they will spread out on the tray.

**bake**           **20min**
... until crisp on the outside and dry in the centre. If you feel they need to be dried out a little more make a slit on the side of each one then dry them out in the warm oven.

Once they are cool whip the cream and fill each bun using either a spoon or piping bag. Make the chocolate sauce below and spoon it over each bun.

| CHOCOLATE SAUCE | | |
|---|---|---|
| cocoa powder | 1tbs | 1tbs |
| castor sugar | 30g | 1oz |
| water | 2tbs | 2tbs |
| icing sugar, sieved | 170g | 6oz |
| cream, whipped | 2tbs | 2tbs |

Put the cocoa power, castor sugar and water into saucepan and stir over an low heat to dissolve the sugar.

Stir in the icing sugar until combined then do the same with the whipped cream.

You can use this chocolate sauce with other cakes (or anything for that matter). It is great in the centre of a sponge with some extra whipped cream or to cover a chocolate roulade for a very decadent treat.

# LEMON SLICES

These squishy, zesty squares are probably our most popular cake. They are rich and beautifully flavorsome with a lightly crisp base and a soft curdy topping. Originally from a Hungarian recipe, these very special lemony squares were developed by Monika at the Café. Some customers request the crust, others want the centre cuts, as if ordering rare, medium or well done. Personally, I like my lemon slices rare! It is the recipe everyone seems to have been waiting for — so here it goes:

| oven | 180°C | 350°F G4 |
|---|---|---|

**9" square tin, lined with baking parchment**

*top*

| plain flour | 250g | 8$\frac{3}{4}$oz |
|---|---|---|
| cold butter, cubed | 250g | 8$\frac{3}{4}$oz |
| icing sugar | 100g | 3$\frac{1}{2}$oz |
| lemon zest | 1 | 1 |
| salt pinch | 1 | 1 |

Mix all the above ingredients together until they form bread crumbs. Pat the mixture down evenly into the tray.

| bake | 20min |
|---|---|

Remove from oven, but do not switch it off just yet.

*bottom*

| eggs | 4 | 4 |
|---|---|---|
| salt pinch | 1 | 1 |
| lemon zest | 2 | 2 |
| castor sugar | 300g | 10$\frac{1}{2}$oz |
| lemon juice | 2 (100ml) | 2 (3$\frac{1}{2}$floz) |
| baking powder | 1lvltsp | 1lvltsp |
| plain flour | 50g | 1$\frac{3}{4}$oz |

Beat the eggs, salt, zest and sugar until foamy and white, and doubled in volume. Add the other ingredients; don't beat at this stage just mix together. Do not overbeat the topping or it will turn out more like a meringue than the curdy texture you are looking for.

Pour on top of the slightly cooled first layer.

| bake | 20min |
|---|---|

If it still wobbles, give it another couple of minutes.

Remove. Cool. Slice into special rectangles. Eat.

There is something very homely about traybakes, there are none of the iced frills, just good solid taste.
I was lucky to grow up in a house where baking was taken for granted. My mother was always popping a tray into the oven or taking a cake tin out. Traybakes are perfect family food as you can cut the squares up as small or large as you like and hide them away in a tin until tea time.

# TRAY BAKES

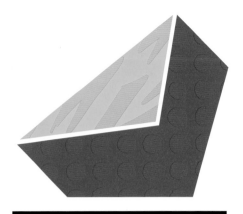

# D A T E C H O C O L A T E
# & G I N G E R
## S L I C E S

| oven | 180°C | 350°F | G4 |
|---|---|---|---|
| 9" square tin, lined with baking parchment | | | |

| water | 330ml | 11floz |
|---|---|---|
| chopped dates | 260g | 9oz |
| plain flour | 175g | 6oz |
| baking powder | 0.5 tsp | ½ tsp |
| light brown sugar | 150g | 5¼oz |
| ground ginger | 3tsp | 3tsp |
| porridge oats | 100g | 3½oz |
| salt pinch | 1 | 1 |
| butter, cubed | 175g | 6oz |
| chocolate chips | 100g | 3½oz |

Put the chopped dates into a saucepan with the water and simmer for about 10 minutes or until the mixture is soft and thick, stirring occasionally. Remove from the heat and cool.

Sift the flour and baking powder into a large bowl. Add the sugar, half of the ginger, oats and salt and mix well.

Add the butter and rub it in with your fingertips until moist clumps form.

Press half the mixture into the base of the lined tin and smooth it out, then spread the cooled date mixture on top: smooth this out too. Sprinkle the chocolate chips over the dates

Spread the remaining oat mixture on top and press down gently with your hands. Sprinkle the rest of the ginger over the top.

**bake**      **40min**
... or until golden.

# G I N G E R
# B R E A D

For me, gingerbread, with its softness, its richness and its faint hint of spices from far-off lands remains to this day my favorite cake. It may not be the prettiest of cakes but it never fails to cheer me up. The first bite brings with it memories of arriving home from school with ice cold hands and shoulders aching from a heavy bag and a warm wedge of dark and sticky ginger bread with a layer of crisp icing on top waiting to cheer me up. Now that I am all grown up I love a slice with a strong, sweet, black coffee.

This gingerbread is better if you make it a day or two in advance of eating.

| oven | 180°C | 350°F | G4 |
|---|---|---|---|
| 9" square tin, lined with baking parchment | | | |

| self-raising flour | 230 g | 8oz |
|---|---|---|
| bicarbonate of soda | 1lvltsp | 1tsp |
| ground ginger | 1hpdtbs | 1tbs |
| ground cinnamon | 1lvltsp | 1tsp |
| mixed spices | 1lvltsp | 1tsp |
| cold butter, cubed | 110g | 4oz |
| brown sugar | 110g | 4oz |
| treacle | 110g | 4oz |
| golden syrup | 110g | 4oz |
| eggs | 1 | 1 |
| milk | 280ml | 9½floz |
| sultanas or | | |
| crystallised ginger | | |
| or candied peel | 100g | 3½oz |

Put flour, spices, soda and butter into a bowl, and mix until they form fine breadcrumbs. Add sultanas, or ginger or peel.

In a saucepan, gently warm milk, sugar, treacle and golden syrup together, stir occasionally, until the sugar dissolves. Lightly mix it with the flour mix, then add the eggs, and beat on speed 1 until it is smooth. Pour into your prepared tin.

**bake**      **50min**

We ice gingerbread with royal icing (p.37) that has been diluted with lemon juice to make it runny.

*TRAY BAKES*

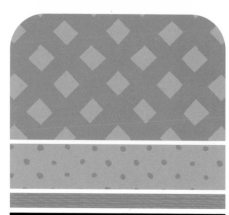

# CHOCOLATE
## B I S C U I T
## C A K E

Digestives, amaretti or ginger nuts are good for this.

**9" square tin, lined with baking parchment**

| | | |
|---|---|---|
| chocolate | 225g | 8oz |
| honey | 150g | 5¼oz |
| butter | 275g | 10oz |
| broken biscuits | 400g | 14oz |
| chopped dried apricots | 40g | 1½oz |
| ground ginger | 1tsp | 1tsp |
| raisins | 40g | 1½oz |
| dried cranberries | 40g | 1½oz |
| chopped hazelnuts | 40g | 1½oz |
| chopped pecan nuts | 80g | 3oz |

Melt the chocolate, honey and butter in a bowl. Stir the mixture and make sure the three ingredients are combined.

Mix in the rest of the ingredients and pour the mixture into the tin.

Allow to cool and then place in the fridge to set. It will take a few hours so perhaps it is best to make the cake the day before.

# APRICOT&
# ALMOND
## S L I C E S

My next-door neighbour Carol used to make this when we were small and she would store small squares in a biscuit tin. Myself and Gemma, her daughter, used to sneak a slice when no one was looking, and nothing ever tastes as good as clandestine cake.

| oven | 180°C | 350°F G4 |
|---|---|---|
| **Swiss roll tin, lined with baking parchment** | | |
| butter | 170g | 6oz |
| castor sugar | 170g | 6oz |
| ground almonds | 110g | 4oz |
| plain flour | 55g | 2oz |
| almond extract | 1tsp | 1tsp |
| eggs | 3 | 3 |
| apricot jam | 280ml | 9½floz |
| puff pastry | 340g | 12oz |

Beat the butter and sugar separately first so they are light and fluffy then stir in the almond, flour and almond extract.

Slowly add the eggs.

Lay half of the pastry onto the swiss roll tin so it covers right to the edges. Spread the jam on top. Pour the almond mixture over and spread it out. Leave about a centimeter around each side.

Cut the remaining pastry into long thin strips and make a lattice over the cake.

**bake**          **35min**
... until golden.

# BROWNIES

We add nuts to our brownies which some people feel is sacreligious. I like the nuttiness and the texture and feel that the chocolate nut combination is a winner. Also we serve a very chocolaty chocolate cake at the café so the nutty brownie provides a very pleasant alternative. If you like, omit the nuts or you can add some raisins, dates or dried cranberries. Brownies can be played around with as you wish.

These brownies can be cooked less if you like them really squishy and sticky. It is a matter of personal taste, so experiment with the length of time you bake them for, to see what you like best. I always err on the side of underdone, as I love a really gooey, sticky brownie.

| oven | 180°C | 350°F | G4 |
|------|-------|-------|-----|
| 9" square tin, lined with baking parchment | | | |

| *melt together* | | |
|-----------------|-----|--------|
| butter | 250g | 8¾oz |
| chocolate chips | 250g | 8¾oz |

| *beat together* | | |
|-----------------|-----|--------|
| eggs | 4 | 4 |
| castor sugar | 333g | 11¾oz |
| plain flour | 150g | 5¼oz |
| chopped nuts *or* **dates** *or both!* | 200g | 7oz |

Mix the two mixtures and pour into lined tray.

| bake | 25–30min |
|------|----------|

... depending on how squelchy you like them!

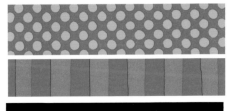

# S P E L T
## & F R E S H F R U I T
## C A K E

### WHEAT FREE

Ripping cuttings from magazines and storing them away is a time-honoured tradition in our family. This recipe was developed from a cutting I took from the *Observer* newspaper. The original recipe had plums but the cake can be made with any type of fresh fruit.

The quantities of the fruit may have to be varied slightly depending on the amount of juice they contain. If you have very ripe and juicy peaches I would use a little less of them as the cake might get very soggy and fall apart. Cherries work really well in this recipe when they are in season.

If you do not have fresh fruit you can soak dried fruit. Prunes in amaretto are particularly good or apricots soaked in brandy. The alcohol will evaporate during the baking of the cake but the flavours will remain.

Spelt is a very ancient grain that is much easier to digest than wheat.

| oven | 180°C | 350°F | G4 |
|------|-------|-------|-----|
| 9" square tin, lined with baking parchment | | | |

| butter | 200g | 7oz |
|--------|------|-----|
| golden sugar | 200g | 7oz |
| eggs | 4 | 4 |
| spelt flour | 150g | 5¼oz |
| baking powder | 2tsp | 2tsp |
| ground almonds | 100g | 3½oz |
| chopped fruit | 500g | 1lb1½oz |
| extra sugar | 1.5tbsp | 1½tbsp |

Cream the butter and sugar until light and fluffy. Lightly beat the eggs and mix into butter slowly.

Mix the rest of the dry ingredients and add to the mixture. Do not overmix or the cake will be heavy.

Spread into tin and scatter plums on top. Shake over the extra sugar.

| bake | 45min |
|------|-------|

... until golden and baked through.

# P E A R S L I C E S

| oven | 200°C | 390°F G5 |
|---|---|---|
| greased & floured Swiss roll tin | | |
| puff pastry | 250g | 9oz |
| butter | 40g | 1½oz |
| castor sugar | 40g | 1½oz |
| eggs | 1 | 1 |
| ground almonds | 50g | 2oz |
| hard pears | 6 | 6 |
| apricot jam | 2tbs | 2tbs |
| lemon juice | 1tbs | 1tbs |

Cover the base of the Swiss roll tin with a sheet of puff pastry and prick with a fork, place in the fridge to cool as you prepare the filling.

Cream the butter and sugar until soft. Add the eggs and almond until it is smooth.

Thinly slice the pears.

Spread the almond cream over the pastry leaving about 1cm around the edge.

Place the slices of pear neatly over the cream in three rows.

**bake          20min**
… until pastry crisp and pears are tender.

Meanwhile heat the apricot jam in the lemon juice until it is simmering and pour over the still warm cake. Slice in three and cut into portions.

# BLACKBERRY & P E A R CRUMBLE

This is my Father's crumble topping recipe. It is quick and easy and makes a tasty dessert. I sometimes sprinkle nuts and brown sugar on top, which makes a wonderful crust. I often use what I call a "lasagne dish" which is 8½×12 inches, but you can use a 9 inch square tin for a deeper crumble. This is a good, big, family size crumble.

| oven | 180°C | 350°F G4 |
|---|---|---|
| oven proof dish, or square tin | | |
| plain flour | 340g | 12oz |
| butter | 270g | 9½oz |
| castor sugar | 55g | 2oz |
| brown sugar | 55g | 2oz |
| oats | 135g | 4½oz |
| amaretti biscuits | 75g | 2½oz |
| blackberries | 340g | 12oz |
| pears, cored & sliced | 600g | 1lb5oz |
| honey | 2tbs | 2tbs |

Beat together the flour, butter and sugar until the mixture forms crumbs. Do not over beat as it will start to combine too much. Roughly crush the amaretti biscuits, and stir them in to the crumbly mixture along with the oats.

Layer the pears and blackberries in an oven proof dish. Drizzle each layer with a little honey. It is really hard to say exactly how much as fruit can vary in sweetness so much. You can trust yourself on this one and use as much as you think is necessary.

Top with your crumble mix and sprinkle a little brown sugar over the lot, and some nuts if you like.

**bake          20min**
… until golden brown.

Other crumbles: rhubarb, apple & mince meat, apple & mixed berries, pear & raspberry, plumb & cinnamon.

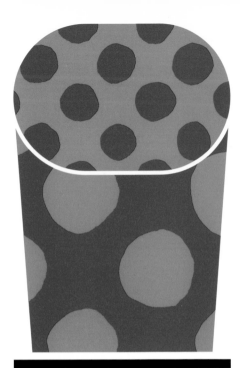

# ORANGE & BLUEBERRY

## DAIRY FREE

This cake also works wonderfully with chocolate chips in place of blueberries.

| | | | |
|---|---|---|---|
| oven | 180°C | 350°F | G4 |
| 2lb loaf tin, lined with baking parchment | | | |
| self-raising flour | 335g | 11¾oz | |
| castor sugar | 185g | 6½oz | |
| orange zest | 2 | 2 | |
| orange juice | | | |
| *or* elderflower cordial | 225ml | 7½floz | |
| eggs | 3 | 3 | |
| light olive oil | 4.5tbls | 4½tbls | |
| blueberries | 150g | 5¼oz | |

Sieve the flour and castor sugar and stir in the orange zest.

In a separate bowl beat orange juice, eggs and olive oil. When this is well blended, add to the dry ingredients. Stir in the blueberries. Pour into tin.

| | |
|---|---|
| bake | 45min |

These cakes can very easily be made without a mixer: just stir the ingredients with a wooden spoon. We use 2lb loaf tins for all of these recipes.

# LOAF CAKES

# BANANA BREAD

My mother used to make this for our school lunches when we were young. It is a great way to use up over-ripe bananas. The riper they are the moister the cake. It is worth asking your local fruit shop for some bananas that are just on the far edge of ripeness, they will often give them to you for free.

If you are using glacé cherries, it is advisable to soak them in warm water, then pat them dry. This will remove some of the sugar and also help prevent them from sinking in the cake.

There are two varieties in this recipe: a cake with cranberries and chocolate or another with sultanas and cherries.

| oven | 180°C | 350°F | G4 |
|---|---|---|---|
| 2lb loaf tin, lined with baking parchment | | | |
| self-raising flour | 225g | 7½oz | |
| salt | 0.5lvltsp | ½lvltsp | |
| butter | 100g | 3½oz | |
| castor sugar | 175g | 6oz | |
| sultanas | | | |
| or dried cranberries | 100g | 3½oz | |
| chopped walnuts | 25g | ¾oz | |
| glacé cherries | | | |
| or chocolate chips | 100g | 3½oz | |
| eggs | 2 | 2 | |
| bananas, mashed | 450g | 16oz | |

Sift flour and salt; rub in butter until it looks like large breadcrumbs. Add sugar, sultanas, walnuts and cherries. Mix together and make a hollow in the centre.

Crack in the eggs and mashed banana. Beat all ingredients thoroughly.

Pour in mixture into your tin and spread it evenly.

**bake**          **1hr30min**

Cool before removing from tin. This cake keeps really well for a few days.

# CARROT CAKE

DAIRY FREE

Our carrot cake has changed and evolved over the past three years. We have finally settled on this recipe. We use light olive oil in place of butter.

| oven | 180°C | 350°F | G4 |
|---|---|---|---|
| 2lb loaf tin, lined with baking parchment | | | |
| self-raising flour | 200g | 7oz | |
| castor sugar | 260g | 9oz | |
| baking powder | 1.5tsp | 1½tsp | |
| mixed chopped nuts | 55g | 2oz | |
| ground cinnamon | 2tsp | 2tsp | |
| ground ginger | 2tsp | 2tsp | |
| raisins | 50g | 1¾oz | |
| light olive oil | 225ml | 9oz | |
| grated carrots | 225g | 7oz | |
| eggs | 3 | 3 | |
| vanilla extract | 2tsp | 2tsp | |

Sift flour into a bowl and mix with the rest of the dry ingredients. Add the olive oil and grated carrot and stir.

Add the eggs one at a time and stir. Finally add the vanilla extract and stir once more. Pour the mixture into your tin and spread it evenly.

**bake**          **1hr15min**

Stick a skewer into the centre, if it comes out clean the cake is cooked, if not put it back into the oven for intervals of 5min.

Cool before removing from tin. Ice and decorate as you wish, we top our carrot cake with cream cheese icing (p.38).

# COFFEE & WALNUT

| oven | 180°C | 350°F G4 |
|---|---|---|
| 8" round tin, lined with baking parchment | | |
| soft butter | 225g | 8oz |
| castor sugar | 225g | 8oz |
| self-raising flour | 225g | 8oz |
| baking powder | 2tsp | 2tsp |
| finely chopped walnuts | 100g | 4oz |
| eggs | 3 | 3 |
| strong espresso, cup | 1 (40ml) | 1 (1.33floz) |

Place the softened butter and the castor sugar into your mixing bowl and beat with the whisk attachment until the mixture is light and fluffy.

In another bowl, combine your other ingredients. Add these to your butter and sugar mix and combine slowly. Scrape into your prepared tin.

**bake**           **35min**
… or until a skewer comes out clean.

The coffee buttercream icing works best with this cake. Oh, how I love coffee buttercream! I usually put a layer through the centre and then cover the outside completely (p.38).

Moni was the first staff member at The Cake Café. I owe her a debt of gratitude — she kept the ovens warm and the cakes baked to perfection as I ran around desperately trying to arrange accounting details and organise phone lines.
So thanks again Moni for all the beautiful cakes.

# CAKE CAKES

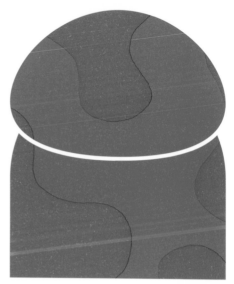

# SPONGE

DAIRY FREE — UNLESS YOU FILL WITH CREAM!

What can I say about a traditional sponge? To me it is the simplest yet most glorious of cakes. A slice of squishy sponge with freshly whipped cream and some homemade jam (or lemon or orange curd) is always a real treat. It still never ceases to amaze me that three simple ingredients can be transformed into something utterly different. This sponge sums up what baking is all about: a strange, mysterious, tasty, fun and delicious science!

| oven | 180°C | 350°F | G4 |
|---|---|---|---|
| **8" round tin, lined with baking parchment** | | | |
| castor sugar | 150g | 5oz | |
| eggs | 5 | 5 | |
| self-raising flour | 150g | 5oz | |

Mix your eggs and sugar for ages with the balloon attachment until really light and fluffy. Sieve in the flour and then fold so the mixture does not lose its volume. Pour into tin.

| bake | 20min |
|---|---|

... until it has risen and is nice and golden. Do not open the oven door during the first half of the baking time.

Whip some cream and then cut the cake in half horizontally through the centre. Spread a layer of cream on the bottom half, and then jam on the underside of the top half. Sandwich together. Make some tea, pour a sherry ...

# Le GATEAU
## CHOCOLAT

This is a rich, dense and delicious cake.

| oven | 160°C | 284°F | G3 |
|---|---|---|---|
| **8" round tin, lined with baking parchment** | | | |

*melt the following in a pot*

| chocolate | 200g | 7oz |
|---|---|---|
| butter, cubed | 200g | 7oz |
| espresso shot of coffee | | |
| *plus water up to* | 125ml | 4floz |

*mix together*

| plain flour | 85g | 3oz |
|---|---|---|
| self-raising flour | 85g | 3oz |
| brown sugar | 200g | 7oz |
| castor sugar | 200g | 7oz |
| cocoa powder | 25g | 1oz |

*lightly beat together*

| buttermilk | 75ml | 2.5floz |
|---|---|---|
| baking soda | 0.25tsp | ¼tsp |
| eggs | 3 | 3 |

Melt chocolate, butter and coffee in a pot. Mix dry ingredients and stir in the chocolate mix. Lightly beat buttermilk and eggs and mix with the rest of the ingredients. Pour into tin.

| bake | 1hr20min |
|---|---|

Smother it in chocolate ganache (p.39).

*CAKE CAKES*

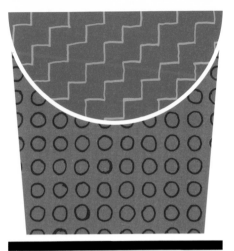

# APPLE &
## CINNAMON

I love a slice of this cake with a cup of tea on a blustery winter's evening. It is comforting and hearty and fills the kitchen with the smell of warm cinnamon ...

| oven | 180°C | 350°F G4 |
|---|---|---|
| 8" round tin, lined with baking parchment | | |

| | | |
|---|---|---|
| soft butter | 225g | 8oz |
| brown sugar | 225g | 8oz |
| eggs | 3 | 3 |
| chopped nuts | 100g | 3½oz |
| raisins | 100g | 3½oz |
| self-raising flour | 225g | 8oz |
| baking powder | 2lvltsp | 2lvltsp |
| cooking apples | 400g | 14oz |
| cinnamon | 1tsp | 1tsp |

Core, peel and grate the apples. Keep aside a handful of chopped nuts and brown sugar to top the cake.

Mix everything except the apples and cinnamon in the mixer. Spread just over half of the cake mixture in the tin. You will need to dip a fork or knife into warm water to help spread the mixture as it is quite sticky.

On top of this spread the grated apple (do not press it into the cake mixture). Dust it with the cinnamon, then top with the rest of the mixture. Scatter a handful of nuts and brown sugar on top of the cake. You can sprinkle a little more cinnamon on top too if you like a stronger flavour.

| bake | 1hr 10min |
|---|---|

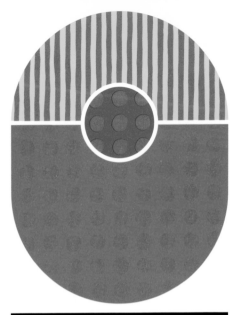

# HONEY &
## RASPBERRY

| oven | 180°C | 350°F G4 |
|---|---|---|
| 8" round tin, lined with baking parchment | | |

| | | |
|---|---|---|
| soft butter | 85g | 3oz |
| sugar | 85g | 3oz |
| eggs | 200g | 7oz |
| ground almonds | 200g | 7oz |
| wholemeal flour | 25g | 1oz |
| baking powder | 1tsp | 1tsp |
| flaked almonds | 50g | 2oz |
| raspberries | a handful | a handful |
| honey | 3-4tbsp | 3-4tbsp |

Put the butter and sugar in a mixing bowl, and cream them together until light and fluffy. Beat in the eggs, one at a time.

Fold in the ground almonds. Sift in the flour and baking powder and gently fold these in.

Scrape half of the mixture into the prepared tin scatter with the raspberries and then smooth on the rest of the mixture: scatter the flaked almonds over the top.

| bake | 45min |
|---|---|

... or until a skewer comes out clean.

Remove from the oven and, while it's still hot, evenly drizzle all over with honey. Serve warm or cold.

*CAKE CAKES*

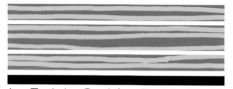

# LEMON CURD CAKE

| oven | 180°C | 350°F G4 |
|------|-------|----------|

**8" round tin, lined with baking parchment**

*for the curd*

| lemon juice & zest | 5 | 5 |
|---|---|---|
| eggs, lightly beaten | 4 | 4 |
| castor sugar | 450g | 1lb |
| butter | 110g | 4oz |

*for the cake*

| natural yoghurt | 225 g | 8oz |
|---|---|---|
| lemon juice | 1tbs | 1tbs |
| lemon zest | 3 | 3 |
| self-raising flour | 175g | 6oz |
| baking powder | 1tsp | 1tsp |
| butter | 50g | 1¾oz |
| castor sugar | 300g | 10½oz |
| eggs, separated | 3 | 3 |

**curd**

Add the lemon juice, zest, eggs, sugar and butter into a heat-resistant bowl. Place the bowl over another larger saucepan that is filled with water. Bring the water to a gentle boil, whisking the curd all of the time. Make sure not to overheat as it will begin to curdle. Remove the curd from the heat once it has started to thicken and coats the back of a spoon with ease. Set aside to cool.

**cake**

Mix the sugar, butter and egg yolks in a bowl. Add the yoghurt and the zest of the lemon, and the lemon juice. Stir until smooth. Gently fold in the flour and baking powder. Whisk the egg whites to a soft peak and carefully fold into the mixture. Pour into the prepared tin.

| bake | 1hr–1hr 15min |
|------|---------------|

Then cool completely. Cut the cake through the centre twice so you have three disks of cake. I use a piece of string to do this. Gently place the string in position around the circumference of the cake and overlap the ends. Pull in opposite directions so it cuts through the cake. Spread two of the disks generously with the lemon curd and then place all three on top of each other so the curd is sandwiched between each layer. Lemon butter cream icing (p.38) is good on this cake.

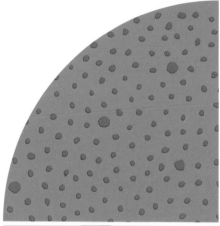

# ORANGE

| oven | 170°C | 300°F G2 |
|------|-------|----------|

**8" round tin, lined with baking parchment**

| soft butter | 250g | 9oz |
|---|---|---|
| orange zest | 4 | 4 |
| sugar | 330g | 11½oz |
| eggs | 4 | 4 |
| self-raising flour | 225g | 8oz |
| plain flour | 75g | 3oz |
| orange juice | 180g | 6oz |

Beat butter, zest and sugar until light and fluffy. Add the eggs slowly one at a time. Slowly mix in the flour and juice. Scrape into your tin.

| bake | 1hr |
|------|-----|

... or until a skewer comes out clean.

I often pour Grand Marnier orange liqueur over this cake while it is still warm for an extra treat. Glace icing (p.37) or an orange butter cream or even cream cheese icing (p.38) would all be delicious.

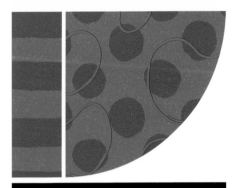

# AOIFE'S GRANNY'S
# CHERRY & ALMOND CAKE
## WITH A DASH OF WHISKEY

This is a cake is best eaten with a big pot of tea!

| oven | 160°C | 320°F G3 |
|------|-------|----------|

8" round tin, lined with baking parchment

| | | |
|------|------|------|
| butter | 170g | 6oz |
| castor sugar | 170g | 6oz |
| eggs | 3 | 3 |
| self-raising flour | 210g | 9oz |
| chopped almonds | 200g | 3½oz |
| cherries | 200g | 3½oz |
| whiskey | 1tbs | 1tbs |
| almond extract | 1tsp | 1tsp |

*whiskey syrup*

| | | |
|------|------|------|
| apricot jam | 4tbs | 4tbs |
| whiskey | 5tbs | 5tbs |

Soak the cherries in the whiskey and add the almond extract.

Cream the butter and sugar. Add in the lightly whisked eggs and sieved flour.

Mix in the soaked cherries and chopped almonds and pour into your lined tin.

**bake**      **40min**

... or until a skewer come out clean from the centre.

When you remove the cake from the oven heat the whiskey and apricot jam until simmering and pour over the warm cake.

# PEACHES & CREAM PIE

| oven | 200°C | 390°F G5 |
|------|-------|----------|

8" tart tin, greased & floured

| | | |
|------|------|------|
| castor sugar | 115g | 4oz |
| plain flour | 40g | 1.5oz |
| vanilla extract | 2tsp | 2tsp |
| lime zest | 1 | 1 |
| cream | 180mls | 6½floz |
| peaches, stoned&halved | 3–4 | 3–4 |
| puff pastry | 280g | 10oz |

Beat together the sugar, flour, vanilla, lime zest and cream until they are completely combined.

Cover the base of the cake tin with the puff pastry trimming any excess from the sides. Pierce with a fork a few times to stop it rising too much.

Fill the pastry shell with the cream mixture. Cover the cream filling with the peaches cut side down. You may have to cut a few into unusual shapes to fit them all in.

**bake**      **40–45min**

... until the cream mixture has set and the pastry around the sides looks golden.

# L E M O N  P E A R
# & P O L E N T A
# C A K E

## WHEAT FREE

| oven | 160°C | 320°F G3 |
|---|---|---|
| 8" round tin, lined with baking parchment | | |
| soft butter | 250g | 8¾oz |
| lemon zest | 2 | 2 |
| sugar | 225g | 8oz |
| eggs, separated | 3 | 3 |
| lemon juice | 0.25 | ¼ |
| ground almonds | 150g | 5¼oz |
| fine polenta | 225g | 8oz |
| pears, cored & sliced | 1 | 1 |
| light brown sugar | 1tbs | 1tbs |
| *for syrup* | | |
| castor sugar | 125g | 4½oz |
| water | 100ml | 3½floz |
| lemon juice & zest | 1 | 1 |

Beat the butter, zest and sugar until light and fluffy. Slowly add the egg yolks, beating well. Stir in the juice, ground almonds and polenta.

Whip the egg whites, until soft peaks form. Carefully fold into the polenta mixture.

Lay the slices of pear on the base of the pan. Fan them out from the centre and sprinkle with a little brown sugar. Then spread the mixture on top.

**bake**      **1hr**
… until a skewer comes out clean.

Meanwhile boil the sugar, water, lemon juice and zest, stirring until the sugar is dissolved. Spoon evenly over the hot cake. When cooled, turn the cake upside down and pour a little more syrup over this side. Excellent eaten warm, with whipped cream or yoghurt. More excellent with limoncello liqueur poured over it!

# O L D  F A S H I O N E D
# A P P L E
# T A R T

| oven | 160°C | 320°F G3 |
|---|---|---|
| 8" tart tin, gresed and floured | | |
| flour | 225g | 8oz |
| cold butter | 140g | 5oz |
| castor sugar | 55g | 2oz |
| eggs | 1 | 1 |
| salt pinch | 1 | 1 |
| apples, cored & sliced | 600g | 1lb5oz |
| sugar | 110g | 4oz |
| mixed spice | 1tsp | 1tsp |

Mix the flour and salt and then rub in butter, do not over mix. Stir the sugar into the egg, mix it lightly and add to the flour.

**rest pastry in fridge**      **3hrs** *or* **overnight**

Gently toss the apple slices in the sugar and mixed spices.

Roll out a circle of pastry to fit in the base of your tin and another than will be used for the top.

Gently let the base circle fit into the edges of the tin. Do not push it out of shape too much but be gentle with it. Prick the base with a fork and fill with the apple mixture. Cover over with the other disk and pinch around the edges so the pieces are stuck. Cut a neat little cross shape in the centre of the tart.

**bake**      **40min**
… until the pastry is golden and you can stick the point of a knife through the slit in the top and it cuts easily through the apple.

# ROULADE

WHEAT FREE

| | | | |
|---|---|---|---|
| oven | 180°C | 350°F | G4 |
| Swiss roll tin, lined | | | |
| dark chocolate | 170g | 6oz | |
| orange juice & zest | 1 | 1 | |
| eggs, separated | 4 | 4 | |
| castor sugar | 140g | 5oz | |

Divide the sugar equally in two.

Melt the chocolate, juice and the zest. Add one half of the sugar, and then the egg yolks.

Meanwhile beat the other half of the sugar with the egg whites. Whip until they form white peaks. Both the bowl and whisk need to be very clean for this because if any fat or grease gets into the mixture the eggs will not fluff up too well. I wipe down the inside of the bowl with a bit of light vinegar to get rid of any residue of butter that may be there.

Gently fold the egg mixture into the chocolate mixture making sure to preserve the bubbles.

**bake**            **20min**
… it is done when it starts cracking on the top.

Turn the roulade onto a clean damp tea towel and leave it to cool. Spread it with cream and orange curd or jam and roll gently when it is still in the tea towel, and on to a plate (see rolling diagram p.9).

# ORANGE CURD
## FOR ROULADE & MORE

Lemon curd is very popular but other citrus fruit also make great curd. I like to put a dash of lemon juice into this recipe but orange makes up the bulk of the flavour. I think it works great with chocolate.

| | | |
|---|---|---|
| butter, melted | 60g | 2oz |
| castor sugar | 130g | $4\frac{1}{2}$oz |
| orange juice | 1 | 1 |
| lemon juice | 0.25 | $\frac{1}{4}$ |
| orange zest | 2 | 2 |
| eggs | 2 | 2 |
| egg yolks | 1 | 1 |

Melt your butter over a low heat. Stir in your sugar, the zest and the juice.

In a bowl lightly whisk your two eggs and extra yolk You need to have them thoroughly mixed together.

Now take the butter mixture off the heat and add in the eggs whisking all the time. When the two are combined you can place the saucepan back on the heat and keep stirring with the whisk or a wooden spoon. I keep the heat on low-to-medium for this part of the process.

You need to keep stirring until the mixture begins to thicken. This may take a while — up to fifteen minutes! It is not easy going but believe me it is worth it, as the saying goes the best things come to those who wait.

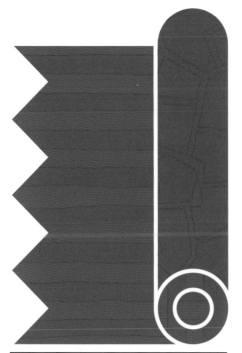

# S W I S S
# R O L L

| oven | 180°C | 350°F | G4 |
|---|---|---|---|
| Swiss roll tin, lined | | | |

| eggs | 5 | 5 |
|---|---|---|
| castor sugar | 150g | 5oz |
| self-raising flour | 110g | 4oz |
| cocoa powder | 25g | 1oz |

Beat eggs and the sugar until white, thick and creamy.

Sieve flour and cocoa powder together, then fold in with a large spoon. Pour into tin.

| bake | 12min |
|---|---|

Sieve sugar onto a clean, dry tea towel. Turn the flat Swiss Roll onto the towel. Cut four nicks towards each end (see rolling diagram p.9), do not cut right through. Roll the Swiss Roll up in the tea towel and leave to cool. When cooled, unroll gently and trim edges for a neat finish. Fill with jam and cream. Roll up again and dust with icing sugar.

# GRANNY NORA'S
# PORTER
# CAKE

This is my Granny Nora's cake recipe. I found it hand written in one of her baking books in her precise and elegant script. It had faded and become difficult to read over the years so I am honoured to be able to put it into print, saved for posterity.

I wrap a double layer of brown paper around the outside of the cake tin and tie with twine to stop the sides of the cake drying out. Cut two discs of the same paper and place one resting on top of the cake, the other underneath the tin on the shelf of the oven.

| oven | 145°C | 290°F | G1½ |
|---|---|---|---|
| 8" round tin, greased & lined with baking parchment | | | |

| dried fruit | 450g | 1lb |
|---|---|---|
| stout | 250ml | 8½floz |
| butter | 225g | 8oz |
| brown sugar | 225g | 8oz |
| plain flour | 340g | 12oz |
| eggs | 2 | 2 |
| chopped nuts | 55g | 2oz |
| treacle | 2tbs | 2tbs |
| mixed spices | 2tsp | 2tsp |
| lemon juice & zest | 0.5 | ½ |
| salt pinch | 1 | 1 |
| bread soda | 0.5lvltsp | ½lvltsp |

Soak the fruit in half of the stout.

Cream butter and sugar. Add treacle, eggs and half of the stout slowly, add the flour. Mix in the fruit and spices. Mix well. Lastly mix the bread soda with the remaining stout and mix this in.

Pour into the prepared tin.

| bake | 45min |
|---|---|

stick a skewer in and see if it comes out clean. It may take a good bit longer than the initial 45 minutes, as every oven is different. Keep an eye on it and test ever ten minutes or so making sure the skewer is completely clean before removing the cake from your oven.

Cool in the tin.

# BAKED ALASKA

I think the poor old Baked Alaska has got a bad rap over the years. The blame I place solely at the feet of dodgy hotel banquets serving up cheap whiter-than-white ice cream covered in over-sweet meringue. So use the best quality vanilla ice cream you can get. The meringue insulates the ice cream, stopping it from melting for the short time it is in the hot oven. I guarantee you if you try this recipe you will be hooked and it is easier than you think.

| SPONGE | | | |
|---|---|---|---|
| oven | 180°C | 350°F | G4 |
| 8" round tin, lined with baking parchment | | | |
| self-raising flour | 85g | 3oz | |
| eggs | 3 | 3 | |
| castor sugar | 85g | 3oz | |

Beat the eggs and sugar until light and fluffy. Fold in the flour gently. Pour into cake tin.

**bake**            **8–10min**

If you press the middle of the sponge lightly with your finger it springs back up it is ready. Take it out of the tin straight away and leave to cool.

| FRUIT MIX | | |
|---|---|---|
| blueberries | 125g | 4½oz |
| raspberries | 125g | 4½oz |
| castor sugar | 0.5tbs | ½tbs |

Stew fruit gently for 5 minutes and then stir in the sugar. Leave until cold.

| MERINGUE | | |
|---|---|---|
| egg whites | 3 | 3 |
| castor sugar | 85g | 3oz |

Beat the egg whites until stiff. Beat in the castor sugar.

| ICE CREAM | | |
|---|---|---|
| vanilla ice cream | 450g | 1lb |

| ALASKA! | | | |
|---|---|---|---|
| oven | 220°C | 420°F | G7 |

When you are ready to serve your Baked Alaska put the sponge onto a baking tray. Pour over fruit and the juice making sure it is all on the sponge on not the tray. Cover generously with the ice cream.

Completely cover the ice cream with the meringue.

**bake**            **4–5min**

The peaks of the meringues will brown slightly. Serve immediately.

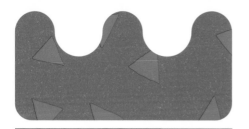

# PAVLOVA

## DAIRY & WHEAT FREE
## DEPENDING ON FILLING!

Anna Pavlova was a Russian ballerina, famous for her role as The Dying Swan at the start of the 20th century. This dessert was created in her honour in the 1920s. What a delicious way for your name to live on — *eat me!*

| oven | 130°C | 266°F | G¾ |
|------|-------|-------|-----|

**baking tray, cut a piece of baking parchment to fit the tray, then cut this down centre**

| egg whites | 6 | 6 |
|------|-------|-------|
| salt pinch | 2 | ouch! |
| castor sugar | 310g | 11oz |
| cornflour | 2tsp | 2tsp |
| white malt vinegar | 2tsp | 2tsp |

Crack the eggs one at a time as any yolk that gets into the mix will affect how the meringue whisks and sets. Put egg whites and salt into a very clean mixing bowl. Whisk lightly until the colour begins to change to white.

Add ½ the castor sugar and whisk until stiff.

Turn the speed on the mixer down and add the rest of the sugar a tablespoon at a time.

Add cornflour and beat, add vinegar and beat.

Scoop the mixture onto the parchment and make an indentation in the centre and swirl the edges.

| bake | 15min | | |
|------|-------|-------|-----|
| reduce heat to | 120°C | 248°F | G½ |
| bake further | 1hr30min–2hr | | |

... depending on your oven. Watch carefully so it does not get too brown (if you have a glass door) but do not open the oven!

When the meringue is done it should slide off the baking tray onto a plate. You can then pull the paper gently out from underneath on both sides. Because it is cut in two it should pull away easier. Traditionally, pavlova is filled with freshly whipped cream and then topped with summer berries.

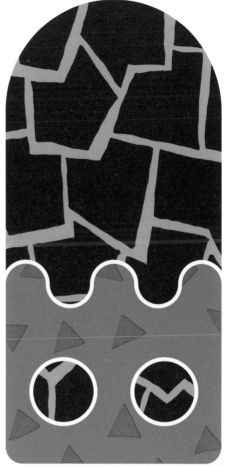

# CHOCOLATE PAVLOVA FILLING

| cream | 300ml | 10floz |
|------|-------|-------|
| chocolate | 200g | 7oz |

Whip the cream until stiff.

Melt the chocolate in a double pot but make sure not to allow any steam into the chocolate. Put a tablespoon of cream into the chocolate and stir the two together.

Pour the chocolate mix into the cream quickly before it starts to harden. If the mixture is too runny put it in the fridge for a bit. Fill Miss Pavlova with the chocolate cream!

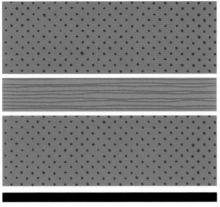

# S P I C E D
# R H U B A R B
# C A K E

Rhubarb grows really well in Ireland and is a wonderfully versatile fruit. You can also use it in the crumble recipe or simply stewed and served with warm, creamy, vanilla-flecked custard.

| oven | 160°C | 320°F G 3 |
|---|---|---|
| 8" round tin, greased & lined with baking parchment | | |
| soft butter | 170g | 6oz |
| castor sugar | 170g | 6oz |
| self-raising flour | 170g | 6oz |
| ground almonds | 170g | 6oz |
| ground ginger | 1.5tsp | 1½tsp |
| eggs | 1 | 1 |
| egg yolks | 1 | 1 |
| rhubarb | 450g | 1lb |
| castor sugar | 40g | 1½oz |

Stew the rhubarb over a low heat in a saucepan with a lid on until soft. Keep an eye on it and stir occasionally. It will create its own, tangy pink juices. Stir in the sugar and continue stewing until it has melted. Leave to cool completely.

Beat the butter and sugar until thick and creamy. Beat in the egg and egg yolk. Fold in the sieved flour, ginger and ground almonds.

Pour half of the mixture into the tin.

Spread the cold stewed rhubarb onto the mixture.

Cover with the remainder of the cake mixture.

| bake | 65min |
|---|---|

Let all biscuits cool completely before storing them, otherwise they will go soft. Biscuits should not be stored in the same container as cakes or they will absorb the moisture from the cakes and begin to soften.

# BISCUITS

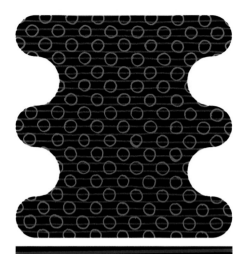
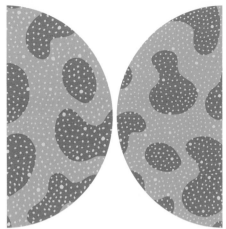

# GINGER HUGS

# BUTTER KISSES

We serve these biscuits on a plate with Butter Kisses. They come with chocolate ganache, and some cream scented with cinnamon. They were originally imagined for children — of all ages!

If your ginger hugs start to become too hard you can soften them back up by placing them into an airtight container with a slice of apple.

| makes | around 20 hugs | | |
|---|---|---|---|
| oven | 180°C | 350°F | G4 |
| baking tray, lined with baking parchment | | | |

*mix together*

| egg yolks | 2 | 2 |
|---|---|---|
| plain flour | 450g | 1lb |
| bread soda | 10g | $\frac{1}{3}$oz |
| ground ginger | 15g | $\frac{1}{2}$oz |
| cake spice | 15g | $\frac{1}{2}$oz |

*melt together in a pan*

| treacle | 50g | 1$\frac{3}{4}$oz |
|---|---|---|
| golden syrup | 150g | 5$\frac{1}{4}$oz |
| butter | 80g | 2$\frac{3}{4}$oz |
| brown sugar | 80g | 2$\frac{3}{4}$oz |

Pour the egg mixture into the treacle mixture. Beat until it forms a ball.

It needs to be used quickly or else it crumbles. So roll it straight away to 4–5mm thick. Cut into "hugs" ("O").

| bake | 8–9min |
|---|---|

These biscuits can be cut into what ever shape takes your fancy. There are hundreds of different cutter shapes available.

| makes | around 60 little kisses | | |
|---|---|---|---|
| oven | 180°C | 350°F | G4 |
| baking tray, lined with baking parchment | | | |

| butter | 200g | 7oz |
|---|---|---|
| castor sugar | 200g | 7oz |
| eggs | 1 | 1 |
| lemon juice | 2tbs | 2tbs |
| vanilla extract | 1tsp | 1tsp |
| plain flour | 500g | 1lb1$\frac{1}{2}$oz |
| baking powder | 1tsp | 1tsp |

Beat the butter and sugar until fluffy.

Then mix in the egg, lemon juice, and vanilla extract. Finally beat in the flour that has been mixed with the baking powder.

When the dough is coming together, take it out of the machine, knead lightly into a ball, wrap it in cling film, and leave in the fridge for an hour.

Roll out into 3–4mm thick, then cut with your chosen cutter.

| bake | 7–8min |
|---|---|

… until they are nicely brown.

Decorate with coloured icing (p.39). Dry the iced biscuits in the still-warm oven.

# SWIRLY
## CHOCOLATE
## FILLED FINGERS

### EGG FREE

| | | |
|---|---|---|
| makes | around 12-15 fingers | |
| oven | 190°C | 375°F  G5 |
| piping bag fitted with a large star nozzle | | |

| | | |
|---|---|---|
| butter | 120g | 4oz |
| icing sugar | 30g | 1oz |
| plain flour | 120g | 4oz |
| baking powder | 0.25lvltsp | ¼lvltsp |
| vanilla extract | 4 drops | 4 drops |
| chocolate | 60g | 2oz |
| icing sugar | for dusting | |

Beat the butter until it is smooth then beat in the icing sugar until the mixture is pale and fluffy.

Sieve in the flour and baking powder. Beat well then add the vanilla until combined.

Using the large star nozzle, pipe the mixture the length of your fingers onto a lined baking tray, keeping them all relatively the same length. Pipe slowly, zig-zagging along the way to make the lengths wider.

| | |
|---|---|
| bake | 7min |

... until lightly golden.

Cool on a wire rack.

Melt the chocolate over some hot water and gently dip the ends of each biscuit into the chocolate. Leave to cool again.

### CHOCOLATE FILLING

| | | |
|---|---|---|
| soft butter | 65g | 2¼oz |
| icing sugar | 120g | 4¼oz |
| chocolate, melted | 1tbs | 1tbs |

Beat the butter until it is as white as possible. Beat in half the icing sugar.

Stir in the rest of the icing sugar and melted chocolate with a wooden spoon.

Cover the base of half of the biscuits with the filling and sandwich together.

# ORANGE
# MELTS

| | | |
|---|---|---|
| makes | 16 | |
| oven | 160°C | 320°F  G3 |
| baking tray, lined with baking parchment | | |

| | | |
|---|---|---|
| butter | 220g | 7¾oz |
| icing sugar | 110g | 4oz |
| orange zest | 2 | 2 |
| plain flour | 220g | 7¾oz |
| corn flour | 55g | 2oz |
| salt pinch | 1lrg | 1lrg |

Mix your butter and sugar until they are pale in colour.

Meanwhile sieve your flour, cornflour and salt. Add these ingredients and the orange zest to your butter and sugar. I find it best to combine all of these with my hands until they form a dough. Do not worry if it looks a little dry: it will come together in your hands.

Roll your dough into 16 small ping-pong balls, and place on a baking tray lined with parchment. Leave space between each one, as they will spread.

Press each ball with the back of a wet fork or spoon.

| | |
|---|---|
| bake | 15min |

Leave to cool for a few moments when they come out of the oven then transfer them onto a wire rack.

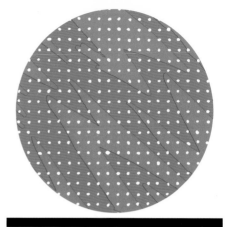

# L A D Y
# G A A
# B I S C U I T S

# O A T
# B I S C U I T S

You can vary the contents of these biscuits. We generally use a mixture of nuts or chocolate chips or sometimes raisins. You can divide the batch up and use a portion of each. Glacé cherries, crystallised ginger, dried apricots or prunes all work.

| makes | 18 | | |
|---|---|---|---|
| oven | 180°C | 350°F | G4 |
| baking tray, lined with baking parchment | | | |

| soft butter | 250g | 8¾oz |
|---|---|---|
| castor sugar | 50g | 1¾oz |
| light brown sugar | 100g | 3½oz |
| self-raising flour | 150g | 5¼oz |
| porridge oats | 225g | 8oz |
| choc chips, nuts, etc | 250g | 8¾oz |

Beat butter and sugar until fluffy.

Stir in flour, oats and mix well. Add the chocolate chips or nuts or whatever your extra flavouring is, and mix again.

Roll into logs and refrigerate. The dough will keep in the fridge for up to a week so you can slice a few biscuits off and bake them just before you eat them.

| bake | 15–20min |
|---|---|

... until they are turning golden.

My husband is an avid Gaelic football player. When his team got into the semi-final of the championship I thought it was about time that he started eating a healthier alternative to his normal biscuit. I developed these biscuits from our original oat biscuit recipe at the Café. They contain no refined sugar and no wheat flour. I added a mixture of seeds and nuts. There are many possibilities — cocoa, orange zest, peanuts, hazelnuts, etc.

| makes | 12 | | |
|---|---|---|---|
| oven | 180°C | 350°F | G4 |
| baking tray, lined with baking parchment | | | |

| butter or | | |
|---|---|---|
| half olive oil & butter | 150g | 5¼oz |
| fruit sugar | 90g | 3oz |
| oats | 130g | 4½oz |
| seeds | 60g | 2oz |
| spelt flour | 90g | 3oz |
| baking powder | 0.5tsp | ½tsp |
| maple syrup | 2tbs | 2tbs |
| chopped nuts | 60g | 2oz |

Beat the butter/oil and fruit sugar until light and fluffy. Stir in the rest of the ingredients.

Form into 12 small ping-pong balls in your hands and place on the lined baking tray. Leave enough room between them so they can spread to about twice their size.

| bake | 20min |
|---|---|

... or until golden.

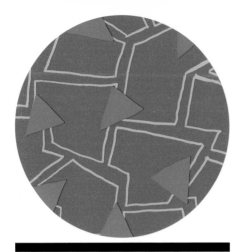

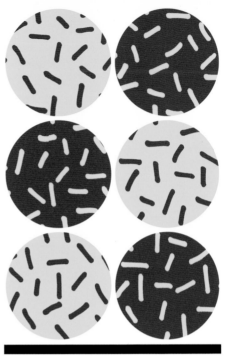

# PEANUT BUTTER CHOCOLATE & SEASALT BISCUITS

| makes | 16 | | |
|---|---|---|---|
| oven | 180°C | 350°F | G4 |

**baking tray, lined with baking parchment**

| butter | 55g | 2oz |
|---|---|---|
| peanut butter | 55g | 2oz |
| castor sugar | 55g | 2oz |
| brown sugar | 55g | 2oz |
| eggs | 0.5 | ½ |
| ground ginger | 1tsp | 1tsp |
| plain flour | 55g | 4oz |
| baking powder | 1lvltsp | 1lvltsp |
| chocolate chips | 25g | 1oz |
| sea-salt pinch | a few generous | |

Beat the butter, peanut butter, and both sugars until combined.

Slowly beat in the egg.

Sift the dry ingredients and beat them in too. Stir in the chocolate chips.

Roll the dough into 16 balls the size of a walnut and place apart on lined baking tray.

Press each one with a fork and sprinkle with some sea-salt.

| bake | 12–15min |
|---|---|

... until golden.

# LEMON & CARAWAY BISCUITS

| makes | 16 | | |
|---|---|---|---|
| oven | 180°C | 350°F | G4 |

**baking tray, lined with baking parchment**

| butter | 110g | 4oz |
|---|---|---|
| castor sugar | 110g | 4oz |
| eggs | 1 | 1 |
| plain flour | 220g | 8oz |
| caraway seeds | 4tsp | 4tsp |
| lemon zest | 4 | 4 |

Beat the butter and sugar until combined. Slowly add the egg.

Sift the flour and add it with the lemon zest and caraway seeds. Keep beating until well mixed.

Roll into 16 small ping-pong balls and place apart on your prepared tray. Press with a fork. Sprinkle some more caraway seeds on each and press with a fork in the opposite direction.

| bake | 10min |
|---|---|

... until golden.

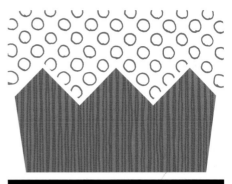

There is great pleasure in icing a cake. You can smooth out all the lumps and bumps that may have occurred in baking and you have freedom to be as creative as you wish.

There are many different types of icing. All delicious. There are no hard and fast rules; this is your cake and you can decide which icing you prefer with which cake.

During the summer months I love to pick some flowers from the garden and use these on top of a cake. A selection of nasturtium and violas work well because you can eat the flowers too.

I find with round cakes it is much nicer to turn them upside down before icing. You then have a smoother surface to work with. If your cake rose in the oven you may need to slice a thin layer off the top before turning it over, otherwise it will wobble.

# ICING

# ROYAL

| egg whites | 3 | 3 |
|---|---|---|
| icing sugar | 450g | 15½oz |
| lemon juice | 2 drops | 2 drops |

Beat the egg white until foamy. Add the icing sugar and beat at a low setting.

Add the drops of lemon juice. Turn up the setting when it is all combined and whisk until fairly stiff.

Dilute with more lemon juice if needed.

If you have any health concerns about eating raw eggs, such as being pregnant or elderly, then use a powdered pasteurised egg white instead, about 17g/½oz should suffice.

# GLACE

| icing sugar | 240g | 8½oz |
|---|---|---|
| soft butter | 2tsp | 2tsp |
| orange juice | 2tbs | 2tbs |

Sift icing sugar in a small pan. Stir in the butter and juice to form a firm paste. Heat it on low heat and keep stirring until icing reaches a spreadable consistency, but do not overheat. Pour it over the cake. It hardens as it cools, so spread it quickly with a wet knife, but let it dribble down the sides.

# ROSE

| icing sugar | 240g | 8½oz |
|---|---|---|
| soft butter | 2tsp | 2tsp |
| rose water | 2tbs | 2tbs |

This is exactly the same as the glace icing above, just with rose water instead of orange juice.

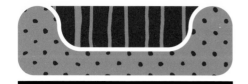

# BUTTER CREAM ICINGS

## VANILLA

| soft butter | 150g | 5¼oz |
|---|---|---|
| icing sugar | 300g | 10½oz |
| vanilla extract | 1tsp | 1tsp |
| milk | 1–2tbsp | 1–2tbsp |

Whip the butter and sugar in a large bowl until very soft, pale and fluffy. Add the vanilla and continue beating.

Beat in the milk, if necessary, to loosen the mixture.

## COFFEE

| soft butter | 150g | 5¼oz |
|---|---|---|
| icing sugar | 300g | 10½oz |
| espresso | 30ml | 1floz |
| milk | 1 drop | 1 drop |

Beat all the ingredients in the mixer with the whisk attachment until light and fluffy. The milk just loosens the mixture slightly and makes it easier to spread.

## LEMON

| soft butter | 150g | 5¼oz |
|---|---|---|
| icing sugar | 300g | 10½oz |
| lemon zest | 3 | 3 |
| lemon curd | 2tbs | 2tbs |
| milk | 1 drop | 1 drop |

Beat the butter and sugar with the whisk attachment until light and fluffy. Add the lemon zest and curd and continue to beat. Add enough milk to loosen the mixture slightly and make it easier to spread.

## CREAM CHEESE

| cream cheese | 100g | 7oz |
|---|---|---|
| honey | 2tsp | 2tsp |
| lemon juice | 1tsp | 1tsp |
| lemon zest | 1 | 1 |
| vanilla extract | 1 drop | 1 drop |
| icing sugar | 50g | 1¾oz |

Mix all of the ingredients with the balloon attachment of your mixer (or just beat it with a wooden spoon) until it is smooth and easy to spread all over your cake.

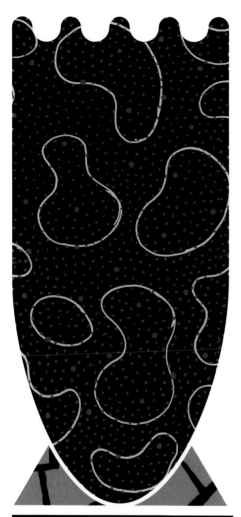

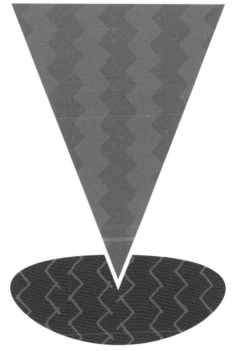

# CHOCOLATE GANACHE

| cream | 150g | 5¼oz |
|---|---|---|
| chocolate | 150g | 5¼oz |

Break your chocolate into bits the size of a penny.

Heat the cream until it is wobbling on top but not quite boiling and add the chocolate. Turn off the heat and stir until the chocolate has melted.

The ganache just needs to be left to cool at room temperature. It should spread like soft butter.

# A RIGHT ROYAL PIPING

To ice our biscuits in the Café, we use royal icing diluted with a little lemon juice until it is smooth enough to pipe easily in thin lines. I have found that the best piping bag to use is a converted freezer bag. I place one corner of the bag into a cup and open it up as wide as possible, fill it with the icing and tie it shut with an elastic band. Now all you need to do is snip a tiny amount off the corner of the bag to make a small hole, and start to pipe.

Divide your icing into batches and add different colours to each. You can then have a few icing bags on the go at the same time for multi-coloured designs. A bag of icing will last a few days in the fridge, so you can always go back to the drawing board ... and, like everything else in this book, you can just eat any of your mistakes.

# THE CAKE CAFÉ BAKE BOOK

**PUBLISHED BY**
MICHELLE DARMODY
&
THE CAKE CAFÉ
DUBLIN
WWW.THECAKECAFE.IE

© 2012 THE CAKE CAFÉ

**DESIGN & ILLUSTRATION BY**
NIALL & NIGEL
PONY LTD
LONDON
WWW.PONYBOX.CO.UK

**PRINT & BIND BY**
MMARTBOOKPRINTING
LUXEMBOURG
WWW.MM-ARTBOOKPRINTING.COM

# THE CAKE CAFÉ DUBLIN

ISBN 978-0-9573212-0-5

HUGS & BUTTER KISSES TO ALL THE AMAZING PEOPLE WHO HAVE MADE THE CAFÉ WHAT IT IS — **M.D.**